Asking Questions Before You Read

When students ask questions before they begin to read, it helps them locate important facts. Thinking about what they want to find out will help them remember important details.

There are different sets of questions that students can use as guides for nonfiction selections. These are provided on reproducible charts on pages 6–8. Before beginning this chapter, you may want to prepare these question charts for each student or create transparencies of each.

End-of-Chapter Challenge

After the class completes the question pages, brainstorm a list of questions for reading about a place and an object. The class can work as a whole or divide into small groups to come up with questions for each topic.

Begin by giving the students some titles to think about. The name of a park, a castle, a city, or a country will help them get started. For an object, suggest the names of inventions, medicines, toys, or machines.

After students formulate their questions, let them try to find the answers in various types of reference materials. Students may find they need to change some of the questions.

Write their sets of questions on charts and post them with the charts for events, animals, and people provided on pages 6–8.

Teacher Tip: Have the students save their activity pages in a portfolio or notebook. They can use the stories several times to practice the many nonfiction skills introduced. They can use the activities as guides when they are working on other school assignments.

Name:

Reading About Events

When newspaper reporters write stories, they try to answer these questions:

Who (are the people in the story)
What (happened)
Where (did it happen)
When (did it happen)
and often they add **Why** (did it happened).

You can use these questions as a guide if you are reading about an event. It could be a story about a basketball game, a Fourth of July parade, or something that happened long ago.

The title of the following story is *The White House Burns*. It is written as if it were an article appearing in a newspaper at the time of the event.

📖 **Before you read about this event, use the five *who, what, where, when,* and *why* words to write a list of questions about this title. The first two questions have been written for you.**

📖 **Leave the line under each question blank so you can fill in the answers after you read the article.**

1. Who burned the White House?

_____

2. What happened when the White House burned?

_____

3. _____

_____

4. _____

_____

5. _____

_____

Reading About Events

The White House Burns

British troops under the command of General Ross and Admiral Cockburn stormed the White House on August 24, 1814. Dolly Madison, the president's wife, fled from Washington City a few hours before the attack. The president was already away.

The British soldiers stuffed souvenirs inside their shirts and uniforms. They piled paintings, draperies, and furnishings in the center of each of the rooms. Even the pianoforte was pushed into the pile.

After the soldiers left the White House, flaming torches, pine poles topped with cotton, were rushed into the president's house. The furniture was set on fire. As the White House went up in flames, the gun powder stored in the basement exploded. The White House was destroyed along with many other buildings in our nation's capital.

Today, Washington City is a mass of rubble, ashes, and debris. The priceless Congressional library has been destroyed. Only the U. S. patent office was saved.

📖 **Answer the *who, what, where,* and *when* questions about this news event without rereading the story. Then reread the article to see if your answers match the information in the story.**

Challenge

- The article does not tell you **why** the British burned the White House.

- Look for information about the War of 1812 in your library. Find out why the United States and Great Britain were fighting a second war. Write the answer under the **why** question.

Name:

Reading About Animals

📖 Study the chart your teacher has provided on *Reading About Animals.* It will help you find information when you read about animals.

📖 Before you read the story about the roadrunner, read the questions that follow the story.

📖 After you have read the story, write the answers to the questions on another piece of paper. If the answer to the question is not in the article, place an X on the line in front of the questions.

The Roadrunner

The roadrunner is a bird that doesn't like to fly. It can use its wings in an emergency, but it prefers to walk. This unusual member of the cuckoo family has loose feathers, a strong bill, and a tail that's longer than its body. The first and fourth toes point backward.

The roadrunner's feathers are streaked brown and buff. There is a featherless line on its cheek that is blue to orange.

The roadrunner hunts rattlesnakes. It stabs the snake with its beak and isn't bothered by the poison. Other popular treats on the roadrunner's menu are grasshoppers, the eggs of other birds, centipedes, scorpions, tarantulas, horned toads, mice, small rats, fruits, seeds, and lizards.

The roadrunner builds a nest in the spring. It chooses a high spot in a cactus or desert bush. The nest is built from snake skins, sticks, roots, leaves, dry manure flakes, and feathers. The female lays three to six white eggs. The male and female birds take turns warming the nest.

_____ 1. The roadrunner is a member of what bird family?

_____ 2. What does the roadrunner look like?

_____ 3. What does the roadrunner eat?

_____ 4. Where does the roadrunner live?

_____ 5. What kind of home or nest does it have?

_____ 6. How does a roadrunner raise its young?

_____ 7. How does a roadrunner protect itself from its enemies?

_____ 8. What interesting habits does the roadrunner have?

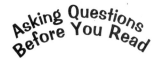

Reading Biographies and Autobiographies

When you read about a person's life, you are reading a biography (the story of a person's life written by someone else) or autobiography (the story of a person's life written by that person). Here is a list of biography questions you can use as a guide:

1. Where and when was the person born?
2. Where and when did the person die?
3. What were the person's early years like?
4. What kind of schooling or education did the person have? (Remember that some people had to learn without schools.)
5. What was interesting or important about the person's life?

Read the story about Matthew A. Henson's life. Write the number of the biography question above the sentence that answers that biography question. For example, 3 would be written by a fact about Henson's early life. Two of the numbers have been written for you. Numbers can be used more than once. Sentences may have more than one number.

Matthew A. Henson, Explorer

①   ③

Matthew A. Henson was born in Maryland. His mother died when he was two and his father died six years later. He moved to his uncle's house in Washington, D.C. His uncle cared for him for a few years and sent him to school.

At thirteen he went to Baltimore and became a ship's cabin boy. The captain of the ship taught him about ships, navigation, geography, and first aid. He traveled all over the world. Wherever he went, he learned about languages and people.

Later, Henson worked on a fishing boat and tried different jobs. Finally, Henson returned to Washington, D.C. He was working as a stock boy in a store when he met Admiral Robert E. Peary. Peary was looking for someone to take part in explorations in the north.

In June 1891, Henson went to Greenland with the admiral. They explored the ice cap. Henson was a valuable member of the expeditions. He worked with Eskimos and he repaired equipment.

Henson was the co-discoverer of the North Pole with Admiral Peary on April 6, 1909.

Reading About Events

Asking questions before you read helps you to locate important facts. Different kinds of stories need different types of questions.

You can often use these questions as a guide when you are reading about an event.

📖 **Who? (are the people in the story)**

📖 **What? (happened)**

📖 **Where? (did it happen)**

📖 **When? (did it happen)**

📖 **Why? (did it happen)**

Reading About Animals

Asking questions before you read helps you to locate important facts. Different kinds of stories need different types of questions.

You can often use these questions as a guide when you are reading about an animal.

📖 **To what family does the animal belong?**

📖 **What does the animal look like?**

📖 **What does the animal eat?**

📖 **Where does the animal live? (habitat)**

📖 **What kind of home does the animal have?**

📖 **How does the animal raise its young?**

📖 **What are its enemies and how does it protect itself?**

📖 **What interesting habits does the animal have?**

 How to Read Nonfiction Books EMC 572

Reading Biographies and Autobiograhies

Asking questions before you read helps you to locate important facts. Different kinds of stories need different types of questions.

You can often use these questions as a guide when you are reading about a person.

📖 **Where and when was the person born?**

📖 **Where and when did the person die?**

📖 **What were the person's early years like?**

📖 **What kind of schooling or education did the person have?**

📖 **What was interesting and important about the person's life?**

Finding Information

When students begin to use the library to find information, locating books can be confusing. It is helpful to take the class to the library for a tour. Small groups need the opportunity to use the library computer or card catalog to locate books.

Following the section on finding information in libraries are activities on finding information in a book.

Library Challenge

After students complete the pages on the library, give pairs of students a list of three subjects, three book titles, and three authors' names. Ask them to find the listings on the library computer or card catalog and print out or list what they find. They can then search for the books in the library. They don't need to take the books off the library shelf unless they want to check them out.

Table of Contents and Index Challenge

Students can have lots of fun using the tables of contents and indexes of textbooks to write questions to stump their classmates. You might create a Question Challenge Box into which students can drop their questions. A question or two can be drawn each day. Award prizes for the toughest questions.

Scanning Challenge I

Give students questions about material in newspapers, magazines, or textbooks. Have them list a few key words and scan for sentences that could answer their questions.

Scanning Challenge II

Have students practice scanning in books about animals. They can look for words about the food different animals eat. Students can make a chart classifying animals by their diets. To begin, have students look for the types of food the echidna and roadrunner eat. Stories about these two animals are in this workbook. To keep the interest level high and students on task, give the class a half hour for their research. When the time is up, they can suggest labels for the chart and put the animal names under the correct labels.

Name:

Where Is It in the Library?

Read the following paragraphs about libraries. Follow the directions given on the second sheet.

Libraries have number or letter systems to help you find the book you need. The computer listings and library catalogs show a number or letter for each book in the library. To help you find books, the library computers have three alphabetical lists. There is a list with the last names of the authors, another one with book titles, and a list of subjects.

The **Library of Congress** and many universities use letters for different subjects. The **Dewey Decimal system,** which many other libraries use, has a system of numbers. The numbers or letters for a book are found in the library catalogs and computer. The shelves in the libraries are numbered or lettered to help you find the shelf with the book you want. Biographies and autobiographies (books about people) are shelved alphabetically by the person's last name. Books for young people often have a J in front of the number. Some books are in a special reference section. You can read them in the library, but you can't check them out.

Libraries have magazines, newspapers videos, tapes, games, movies, and puzzles as well as books. They have microfilm and microfiche machines. Films of books and information can be viewed on these machines.

Name:

Where Is It in the Library?

2

Find It

1. Underline the sentence in the story that tells where you can find the names of books in the library.

2. Circle the way the Library of Congress puts books in order.

3. Draw a box around the way many libraries shelve their books.

4. Draw a triangle in front of the sentence that tells how libraries put biographies in order.

Answer the following questions about libraries.

1. Name the library system that uses numbers.

_____

2. Name two kinds of machines that show books and information on film.

_____

_____

3. List the three ways you can look for books on the library computer.

_____

_____

_____

4. What section of the library has books that can be read in the library, but can't be checked out?

_____

Name:

Dewey Decimal Classification

000 – 099 **GENERAL REFERENCE**	Encyclopedias, bibliographies, computer programming	
100 – 199 **PHILOSOPHY**	Ethics, psychology, philosophy	
200 – 299 **RELIGION**	Different religions, Bible, myths	
300 – 399 **SOCIAL STUDIES**	Government, law, fairy tales, folk tales	
400 – 499 **LANGUAGES**	Dictionaries, sign languages, various languages	
500 – 599 **SCIENCE**	Physics, geology, botany, zoology	
600 – 699 **TECHNOLOGY**	Inventions, medicine, pets, manufacturing	
700 – 799 **ARTS AND RECREATION**	Architecture, crafts, sports, music	
800 – 899 **LITERATURE**	Drama, poetry, humor	
900 – 999 **HISTORY**	Geography, travel, biography	

How to Read Nonfiction Books EMC 572

Name: _____

The Table of Contents

In the front of a nonfiction book are the chapters and chapter titles of the book. The following chapters are for a book about the country of Switzerland.

If you want to find out about the Matterhorn, a famous mountain in Switzerland, and there is no index or listing for Matterhorn in the index, you can look through Chapter 1, beginning on page 4, to see if you can spot information on the Matterhorn.

Decide which chapters listed above have information on the following topics. Write the chapter numbers after the topics.

1. Bern, a city in Switzerland_____

2. Places tourists could visit _____

3. Schools _____

4. Food _____

5. Mountain lakes _____

6. Swiss clocks _____

Inside the Chapter

Some chapters have special headings in black print that help you find a section you need. Under the chapter on cities, for example, you would find a section with the heading, *Bern, City of Bears and Flowers.*

The following are headings found in the chapters listed above. List the chapter number for each set of headings.

1. Fruits and Farm Products, Famous Swiss Cheeses   Chapter _____

2. Visiting the Lakes, Music Festivals, Historic Buildings   Chapter _____

3. Houses, Languages, Work, Entertainment   Chapter _____

Name:

Using the Index

Nonfiction books tell true stories. The stories can be about animals, the weather, places, events, history, science, inventions, people, and sports. Nonfiction books are about the world and the universe. They can answer your questions, help with your schoolwork, and show you how to do things.

Sometimes you want to find information for a report or a test at school. There are other times when you might want to read just to find out about a favorite animal or subject. Most nonfiction books have an index in the back of the book. It lists the topics and the important items the author wrote about in the book. The subjects are in alphabetical order.

Here is a sample index from a book titled *The White House*. On what pages in the book would you find the answers to the following questions? The first question has been answered for you.

---

1. Where does the president work?

14, 26

2. If you were president, where would you and your family live?

_____

3. If the Queen of England were visiting the White House, where would she stay?

_____

4. Is green the only color in the Green Room?

_____

5. How big is the White House?

_____

6. Who designed the White House?

_____

The White House

Index

Additions to, 6, 18, 24, 27
Building materials, 2, 31
Committee for the Preservation of, 36
Cornerstone, 1
Design, 1–2, 13, 15, 26
Dining room, 13
Formal rooms, 6, 13–14
Green room, 14
Guest rooms, 8, 18–20
Hoban, James, 1–2, 13, 15
Johnson, Lyndon B., 14, 36
Kennedy, Jacqueline Bouvier, 40
Official name, 28
Floor plan, 29–30
Porticos, 1–2, 15, 39
Presidents in, 3, 7, 14, 18, 21, 42,
President's office, 14, 26
Reconstruction, 14, 17, 31
Red room, 13
Rooms for the president's family, 7, 15–18
Roosevelt, Theodore, 17, 20
Size of, 1–2, 12, 16, 27
Truman, Harry S., 14, 31

Name:

Tracking Down the Facts

Sometimes there is no table of contents or index. Magazine and newspaper articles are important sources of information without indexes. When you want to find information without these guides, you need to **scan**.

When you scan for information, you don't read every word. Scanning is like looking for a word in a word search puzzle. Here are some steps to follow:

1. Write down or think about **key words** about your subject. For example, if you are trying to find out where an animal lives, you would scan for words like desert and mountains, or the names of countries and continents.

2. When you see a key word, stop and read the sentence carefully. Does it have the information you need? Sometimes a key word answers another question. When that happens, you need to look further for information.

📖 **Scan the following article to:**

1. find out where echidnas live. Circle that sentence.
2. find out what the echidna looks like. Look for color, size, and shape words. Underline these words.

The Echidna

The echidna is a spiny anteater that lives in Australia. Like all mammals, it is a warm-blooded animal with hair that feeds milk to its young. Because it lays eggs, however, the echidna belongs to a special class of mammals called monotremes.

This unusual animal has a long, thin snout, a small mouth, short legs, and spines that cover its back and sides. The echidna's color is brown. Between its spines it has stiff hairs. The toes on the hind feet have long claws.

The echidna is a nocturnal animal that eats ants and termites. This anteater raids ant nests and termite homes. It digs into the nest, pulls out the insects with its long, sticky tongue, and then crushes them in its mouth. Because the echidna has a small mouth with no teeth, grains of dirt that stick to its tongue help grind up the food.

How to Read Nonfiction Books EMC 572

Name:

More Scanning Practice

2

Remember: to **scan** for information, you must have **key words** in mind.

📖 **Underline key words in the following questions. Number one has been done for you.**

📖 **To find the answers, scan the sports article that follows the questions. Write the answers to the questions.**

1. Who made the <u>touchdown</u> for <u>Barkley</u> High?

_____

2. What was the final score of the game?

_____

3. How many touchdowns did Washington score in the last quarter of the game?

_____

4. What is the name of the Washington High team?

_____

5. Who caught five passes in the game?

_____

Washington Upsets Barkley

On Saturday night Washington High trounced football league leader Barkley 41 to 7. Washington scored the first 27 points of the game and added two more touchdowns in the last quarter. The Scorpions' Alan Baker caught five passes and ran 141 yards to keep Washington in the lead. Barkley High, undefeated until they were routed by Washington, scored their only touchdown in the third quarter. Sam Martin ran 23 yards for Barkley's lone TD.

Name:

Scanning a Longer Article

3

You are going to be scanning a story about Granville T. Woods, a great American inventor, to answer some questions about his life.

📖 **Read the first question. A key word has been underlined for you.**

📖 **Scan the article to find the key word. You may need to read the information that comes before and after the key word sentence to find the answer.**

📖 **Write the answer on the line under the question.**

📖 **Repeat the process for questions 2 and 3.**

    1. At what age did Granville Woods go to work for a <u>blacksmith</u>?

    _____

    2. Where did Granville Woods work after he moved to <u>Missouri</u>?
    (Read the sentence after the key word.)

    _____

    3. What did Granville Woods study in night <u>classes</u>?

    _____

📖 **Now you are on your own. Underline key words in the next three questions and see how quickly you can find the answers. Remember: scan for key words; don't read everything.**

    4. What invention did Granville Woods sell to the Bell Telephone Company?

    _____

    5. How did Granville Woods improve train safety?

    _____

    6. What kind of brakes did Granville Woods invent?

    _____

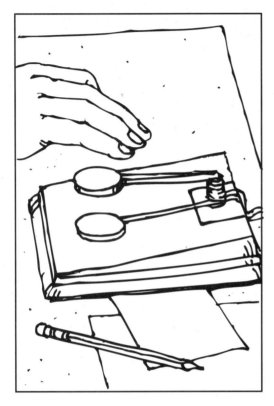

Granville T. Woods

Granville T. Woods was born in 1856 in Columbus, Ohio. He had very little schooling. At age ten he worked as a bellows blower for a blacksmith.

Woods moved with his family to Missouri in 1872. There he worked as a fireman for a railroad. Later he signed on as an engineer on a British steamship.

Woods moved to Cincinnati, Ohio, and opened a machine shop. He manufactured telephone, telegraph, and electrical equipment. He took night classes in mechanical engineering.

In 1884 he improved steam boiler furnaces. He sold his telephone transmitter invention to the Bell Telephone Company of Boston. With the money from the transmitter, he opened the Woods Electric Company.

Many of his inventions improved train safety. He developed a telegraph system that made it possible to send messages between two moving trains. That way, train engineers would know when another train was on the same track. His invention prevented many train accidents.

In 1890 he moved to New York City and spent a lot of his time with his inventions. He developed an electric third rail for streetcars. It reduced friction and made electric rail travel safer. He produced 14 more inventions for electric railways. The automatic air brake system he invented was sold to the Westinghouse Air Brake Company. Another important Woods invention was a safety cutoff device for electrical circuits.

Granville T. Woods, inventions made our lives safer and improved communication systems. He applied for and received more than 50 patents for his inventions.

This chapter shows students how to record and organize the information they find. Activity pages demonstrate mapping information to include main ideas and details. A blank mapping form is provided on page 24.

Creating Information Maps

To help students separate the main ideas and details, the main ideas can be enclosed in boxes and the details placed in circles.

An information map about the roadrunner (page 4) might look like this:

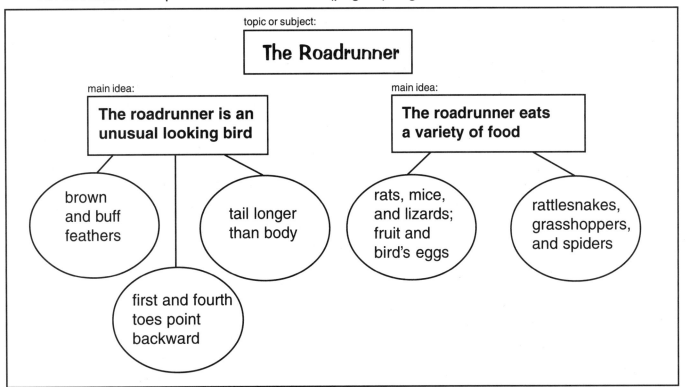

Students can map main ideas and details directly from the information they are reading. To introduce direct mapping, point out the main ideas in paragraphs in social science and science books. Explain that the main idea can be found anywhere in a paragraph, but usually it's at the beginning or end of the paragraph.

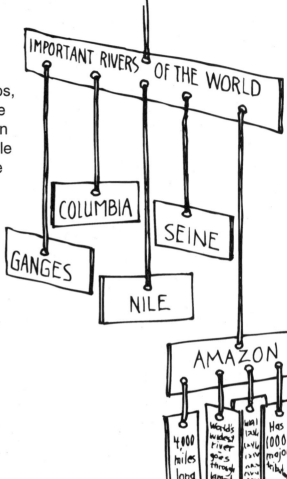

End-of-Chapter Challenge: A River Mobile

Create a "river" mobile that maps information. This project can be done by the whole class, small groups, or individual students. Several mobiles can be made using different rivers so that all students can work on the project. Or you might wish to do the "river" mobile as a model and then let groups or individuals create mobiles on topics of their choice.

Materials needed for each mobile:
- 1 strip of poster board, 24" x 3" (61 x 7.5 cm)
- 5 strips of poster board or construction paper, 8" x 3" (20.5 x 7.5 cm)
- 20 strips of poster board or construction paper, 6" x 2" (15 x 5 cm)
- string
- hole punch
- scissors
- fine tip black marking pens

Steps to Follow:
1. Select five important rivers from a world map.

2. Label the long strip "Important Rivers of the World" and the five shorter strips with the name of each river. Write on both sides so the information can be read from all directions.

3. Record details about each river on four of the shortest strips. Each river will have four facts written about it - eight if you put a different fact on each side of the four strips.

4. Punch holes, tie string, and hang the mobile as shown.

How to Read Nonfiction Books EMC 572

Name:

1

Mapping the Main Idea

An information map is a great way to remember what you read. An information map looks like this:

Topic or Subject
The Amazon River

Paragraph Main Idea	Paragraph Main Idea	Paragraph Main Idea

The **topic** or subject is what you are reading about. For example, the subject for the next story is The Amazon River.

The main idea tells what the paragraph is all about. Everything in the paragraph should be about that idea. Usually the main idea will be in the first or last sentence in the paragraph, but it can be in the middle of the paragraph.

📖 **Read the three paragraphs about the Amazon River. Decide which sentence in each paragraph is the main idea. Underline the main idea sentence. The first one is underlined for you.**

The Amazon River

<u>The Amazon River in South America is one of the world's great rivers</u>. It meanders through the tropical rainforest for 4,195 miles. At times, this slow moving waterway looks more like a lake than a river. When the water level is low, it averages one to seven miles in width. During floods its width can measure 30 miles from one side to the other. The depth of the river ranges from 200 feet to a few inches where sandbars have been formed from sediment in the water. When the water level is high, the Amazon can rise 50 feet above its normal level.

The Amazon has more tributaries than any other river in the world. Rivers from the high Andes Mountains and the the highlands to the north flow into the Amazon. Approximately 1,100 tributaries join the great river. Together, they pour an average of six million cubic feet of water into the Atlantic Ocean every second.

Each day, the Amazon deposits tons of food-laden silt in the ocean. The rotted vegetation in the silt is swept out to sea. It provides food for the fish and plankton in the Atlantic Ocean and the Caribbean Sea. People who live over a thousand miles away eat fish nourished by the Amazon River.

📖 **Write the main idea from each paragraph in the information map boxes at the top of the page.**

Name:

Mapping Information

Using Your Questions

If you have written out questions you want to answer when you read, you can use the answers you find for the main ideas in your map. The following are examples from information about the echidna.

To what family does the echidna belong?

What food does the echidna eat?

topic or subject:

The Echidna

main idea:

The echidna belongs to the family of animals classified as monotremata.

main idea:

The echidna eats ants and termites.

Now You Try It

Here are two questions a student might have asked about black bears. Use the answers to begin an information map. Remember to write the topic, **Black Bears**, in the top rectangle.

What do black bears look like?
   Black bears are the smallest bears in North America

What do black bears eat?
   Black bears are omnivores.

topic or subject:

main idea:

main idea:

Name:

Mapping Information

3

Adding Details

When you read about people, animals, places, events, and objects, you will find many facts about the main ideas. These pieces of information are called **details**. When you want to remember the details, add the information to the main ideas on the map.

Here is the information map you have created on the topic Black Bears. Read the details at the bottom of the page. Write each detail in a circle under the correct main idea.

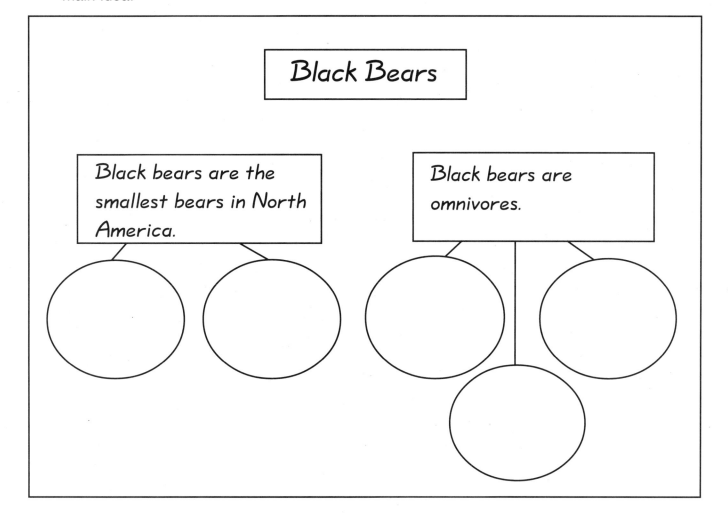

Details

Black bears eat grasses, herbs, and skunk cabbage.
Black bears eat animals that die during the winter.
Females weigh 120 to 180 pounds.
Black bears eat nuts and berries.
Males weigh 250 to 350 pounds.

Mapping Information Form

topic:

main ideas:

Notes and Outlines

Taking Notes

When students are writing reports and finding more information, they need to work with notes and outlines. The questions and information maps they have practiced can be used along with note taking and outlines. To combine questions and note taking, students write each question on a separate piece of paper. The information students find is recorded under the appropriate question. The following examples can be reproduced on a transparency and used to introduce questions and note taking.

Stress to students that when taking notes they need to write the information in as few words as possible.

Sally Student wants to report on spiders. One of the questions she wants to answer is "How do spiders care for their young?" She wrote the question on a piece of paper and recorded the information she found. Notice that she did not write complete sentences.

How do spiders care for their young?
1. many wrap eggs in silk egg sacs called cocoons - protects eggs
2. some stay until babies hatch, not eating
3. some female spiders leave after eggs are in cocoons
4. wolf spider carries cocoon until babies hatch - then they ride on her back.

Sammy Student is going to report on black bears. One of his questions is "What does the black bear look like?" Here is a paragraph that he read and the notes he took.

The front claws of the black bear are shorter and more curved than the claws on the back feet. Unlike those of a cat, the claws are not retractable. The front feet are shaped like the human hand, and the back feet are like the human foot.

Notes:
1. front claws shorter, more curved
2. claws not retractable
3. front feet like human hand
4. back feet like human foot

Note-Taking Challenges

Challenge 1

To quickly introduce a social studies or science chapter, assign a different paragraph or short section to pairs of students. The students write the main idea or question for the selection they read. They then take notes and post the main idea and notes on a chart.

Challenge 2

Assign social studies pages to groups of four students. The students scan the pages for dates. When they find a date, they take notes about the event and fasten the date and notes to a time line with a clothespin. The groups can arrange and change the location of the notes so the line stays in chronological order. When all the groups finish, the dates and notes are glued to a long strip of paper for a class time line.

Outlining

Students working with the activities in this book have learned to use a map to organize the information they read.

Setting up an outline using a map as a guide is a simple way to introduce this important skill. After students are able to outline their notes using a map, they can choose either mapping or outlining to organize information.

Even after students master outlining skills, they may find it easier to continue writing outlines from information maps. Students should continue to use questions or the main ideas of paragraphs to organize outlines and maps.

Page 42 provides a blank outline form that uses Roman numerals and capital letters only. Arabic numerals and letters are not added to the outlines in this book, but they can be introduced by the teacher when the students have mastered the basic outline form.

Name:

Taking Notes

When you need to remember a lot of information for a report, you can take shortcuts. Instead of writing complete sentences, just write enough so you will remember the main ideas and the details. Leave out the unimportant words.

To begin learning about taking notes, read the following story about the reporter Nellie Bly.

Nellie Bly

Elizabeth Cochrane was born in 1867. She was 18 years old when she went to work as a writer for the Pittsburgh Dispatch, a newspaper in Pittsburgh, Pennsylvania. She used the pen name Nellie Bly. (Sometimes authors use pen names instead of their own names.) She wrote about social problems in the city. People read her articles about conditions in the factories and housing for the poor. Her readers helped make changes that improved the lives of many people.

She went to work for the *New York World* newspaper in 1887. She pretended to be mentally ill and was sent to Blackwell's Island asylum as a patient. She found that the patients were mistreated and many people did not belong there. She wrote about her experiences. People were shocked when they learned about the conditions there. Her article brought many needed changes.

On November 14, 1889, Nellie Bly sailed out of New York harbor. She set out to see if she could beat the 80 day around-the-world record of Phileas Fogg. Fogg was a fictional character in Jules Verne's book *Around the World in Eighty Days*. She traveled by ship, train, sampan, horse, burro, stagecoach, and jinricksha. She made the trip in 72 days, 6 hours, 11 minutes, and 14 seconds. In 1890, she wrote a book, **Around the World in 72 Days**.

She married a millionaire, Robert Seaman, in 1895. When he died, she ran his manufacturing plant. The business failed in 1913.

In 1914, Nellie went to Europe. Because of World War I, she was interned there and had to stay until the end of the war.

She went to work for the New York Journal after the war. Nellie Bly died on January 27, 1922.

Name:

Taking Notes

2

📖 **Here are some notes taken from the article about Nellie Bly. Some of the notes do not give enough information. Put an X in front of these notes and rewrite them below. Add details so the facts are complete.**

___ **1.** Born

___ **2.** newspaper writer

___ **3.** Elizabeth Cochrane real name — Nellie Bly pen name

___ **4.** wrote about social problems

___ **5.** her stories caused people to change the way things were done

___ **6.** worked for *New York World* newspaper in 1887

___ **7.** went to Blackwell's Island, an asylum for the mentally ill, as a patient

___ **8.** mistreated

___ **9.** her article helped bring about better conditions

___ **10.** set out Nov. 14, 1889, to beat 80 days around world record of Phileas Fogg, character in Jules Verne novel, *Around the World in Eighty Days*

___ **11.** traveled

___ **12.** returned

___ **13.** married

📖 **On the lines below, rewrite the notes that do not have enough information.**

_____

_____

_____

_____

_____

_____

📖 **Add three notes of your own about Nellie Bly. Make sure you do not repeat any of the details given in notes 1-13. Remember: Use only the words that are needed.**

14. _____

15. _____

16. _____

　　　　　　　　　　How to Read Nonfiction Books EMC 572

Name:

Taking Notes

3

When you take notes, you will often be writing on small cards or in narrow rows on charts where there isn't much room. You need to write only the most important words. Any word that is not necessary for the meaning should be left out. You can use commas and dashes to separate parts of the note.

Rewrite each complete sentence below as it might appear on a note-taking card. The number in parentheses gives the number of words to try for. Number one is done for you.

1. The jaguar, a member of the cat family, has a brownish-yellow coat marked with many dark spots. (7)

   jaguar – cat family – brownish-yellow, dark spots.

2. Sojourner Truth traveled far and wide speaking against slavery, even visiting President Abraham Lincoln at the White House. (8)

   _____

3. The moon is smaller in size than the Earth and covered with grayish rocks and fine dust. (7)

   _____

4. Koalas, whose name means "no drink" in Aboriginal language, are found in eucalyptus forests of the coastal areas of northeastern and southeastern Australia. (11)

   _____

5. Besides being a tasty and healthful food, peanuts can be used to make soap, face powder, shaving cream, shampoo, and paint. (12)

   _____

6. Christopher Columbus was convinced that if he could sail around the globe, he would prove that the earth was a sphere, not flat as many believed. (10)

   _____

7. A rhinoceros rests most of the day and is active at night, when it eats grass, leafy twigs, and shrubs. (11)

   _____

Name:

Note-Taking Practice

4

Sally Student's friend Sarah read a short article about comets. Then she took notes on the article. Sarah didn't know that when you take notes you write only the most important words, so her notes are in complete sentences.

Rewrite Sarah's notes using only the necessary words. The first one has been done for you.

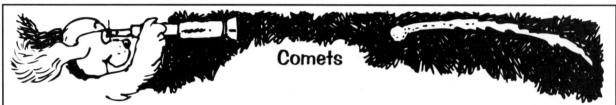

Comets

A comet is a chunk of ice, dirt, and rock. As a comet nears the sun, the ice is melted and then evaporates to form a gas. The gas, dust, and debris jets out away from the comet. It forms a gas cloud called a coma. This coma or tail can stretch out for a million miles. We see the coma when the comet nears the sun.

Comets become millions of tons lighter after a trip around the sun. The dust and gas they lose can be pulled to other planets or drift in space.

Some comets visit the sun once, then shoot out into space. Others, like Halley's comet, make return visits. Halley's comet will be closest to the sun again on July 28, 2061. It takes 76 years for Halley's Comet to complete its orbit.

1. Comets are chunks of ice, dirt, and rock. _made of ice, dirt, rock_

2. The coma or tail is made up of gas. _____

3. A coma can be a million miles long. _____

4. A comet is smaller after traveling around the sun because it loses tons of dust

   and gas. _____

5. Some comets visit the sun once, but others return. _____

6. Halley's Comet returns to the sun every 76 years. _____

7. Halley's Comet makes its next return trip around the sun in 2061. _____

_____

Main Ideas and Details

1

Here is a story about Mount St. Helens, an active volcano in the state of Washington, U.S.A. In both paragraphs the first sentence gives the main idea of that paragraph.

📖 **Read the story. Then follow the directions on page 2 to organize the details under the correct main idea.**

Mount St. Helens Explodes

The eruption of Mount St. Helens on May 18, 1980, caused widespread destruction. Tons of ash, ice, and rock shot out of the volcano. Steam and rock roared 60,000 feet into the air. Lightning bolts and flaming cinders set off forest fires. Nearby Spirit Lake became a boiling mass of mud and debris. Melting snow and ice flowed down the volcano's slopes. Mud slides blocked the rivers and caused floods. Mudflows carried away logs and houses. The mud and debris covered roads, bridges, and buildings.

Signs of the explosion traveled long distances. The eruption blocked out the light of the sun in Spokane, Washington, miles away. Neighboring states were blanketed by falling ash. A light volcanic dust drifted as far away as northern Virginia, settling on cars and houses.

Name: _____

Main Ideas and Details

2

You have read a story about the eruption of Mount St. Helens. The main idea sentence of each paragraph is given. Below that are notes on six details from the story.

📖 **Write the numbers of the details under the main idea where they belong. Number one has been done for you.**

The eruption of Mount St. Helens on May 18, 1980, caused widespread destruction.

_____

Signs of the explosion traveled long distances.

1
_____

---

1. eruption blocked out sunlight in Spokane, Washington

2. steam, rock 60,000 feet up

3. volcanic dust as far as Virginia

4. mud, debris covered roads, bridges, buildings

5. lightning, flaming cinders caused forest fires

6. Spirit Lake mass of mud, debris

📖 **On the lines below, write notes on two more details from the story about Mount St. Helens. Then record each number under the correct main idea.**

7. _____

_____

8. _____

_____

Name:

Outlines

An **outline** is a way of organizing information that can help you write a report or story. In a way it's like a skeleton - it holds a body of information together and keeps it in order.

• At the top of an outline is the title. That's the **heading**.

• Next come the questions or **main ideas** which are written after **Roman numerals**.

• Indented **capital letters** written under the main ideas keep the **details** in order.

• Sometimes there is special information about the details. These facts are numbered.

• Here is a "bare bones" outline.

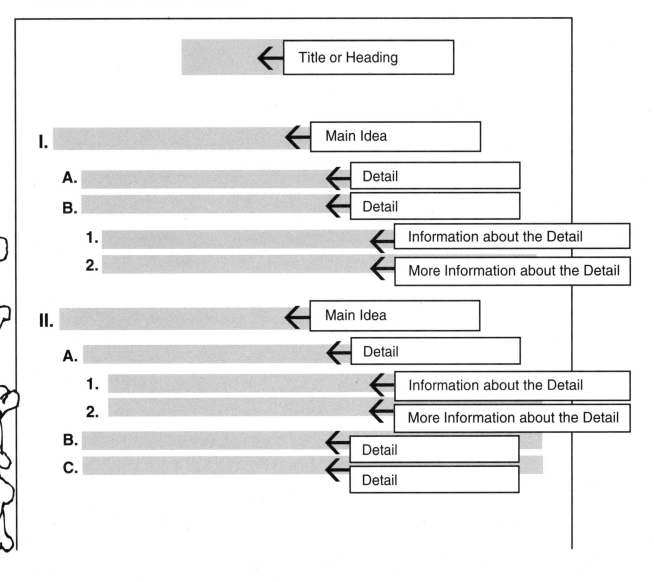

Title or Heading

I. → Main Idea
  A. → Detail
  B. → Detail
    1. → Information about the Detail
    2. → More Information about the Detail

II. → Main Idea
  A. → Detail
    1. → Information about the Detail
    2. → More Information about the Detail
  B. → Detail
  C. → Detail

Name:

Completing an Outline

2

Here is the beginning of a sample outline for a report on the echidna, an Australian animal. Use the information map following the outline to complete section III of the outline.

- Notice that each line begins with a capital letter.
- Write in note form - use necessary words only

The Echidna

I. **Is a monotreme**

   A. **Warm-blooded**
   B. **Feeds its young milk**
   C. **Lays eggs**

II. **Is a spiny anteater**

   A. **Thin snout**
   B. **Small mouth**
   C. **Short legs**
   D. **Spines cover back and sides**
   E. **Stiff hairs between spines**
   F. **Hind feet toes have long claws**
   G. **Is brown**

III. **Eats ants and termites**

   A. _____

   B. _____

   C. _____

   D. _____

The echidna eats ants and termites

- crushes food in mouth - no teeth
- digs up nests and homes of insects
- grains of dirt it scoops up help grind its food
- pulls out insects with long, sticky tongue

Save the outline about the echidna. You will need it later.

How to Read Nonfiction Books EMC 572

Name:

Putting It All Together
Notes, Maps, and Outlines

Sally, Sammy, and Sarah's classmate Stanley Student decided to do a report on Phillis Wheatley, the first African American woman poet to be published.

Stanley read a book and took notes about Phillis Wheatley's life. However, he doesn't think he will get his report done on time without some help on the information map and the outline. This is where you come in:

📖 **Read Stanley's notes**

📖 **Complete his information map on sheet 2**

📖 **Use the information map to complete his outline on sheet 3**

Notes on Phillis Wheatley

Early Life
born in Africa
captured, brought to America as
    slave when 8 or 9
bought by John Wheatley in Boston

Her Poetry
First poem age 13
Wrote poem for Mary's Wedding
Boston people wanted poems written
    for them
Traveled to England - poems published
    in 1773

Life as a Slave
Companion for twins, Mary and
    Nathaniel
Helped Mrs. Wheatley, an invalid
Taught to read and write
Given freedom in 1772 when about 20

Her Later Life
Married John Peters
Had three children, two died
Husband taken to debtors' prison
She and her baby died, December 1784

Name:

Putting It All Together

2

Stanley was planning to make an information map before he wrote an outline. The map would organize the details under the main ideas.

Lend Stanley a hand and make an information map from the notes about Phillis Wheatley.

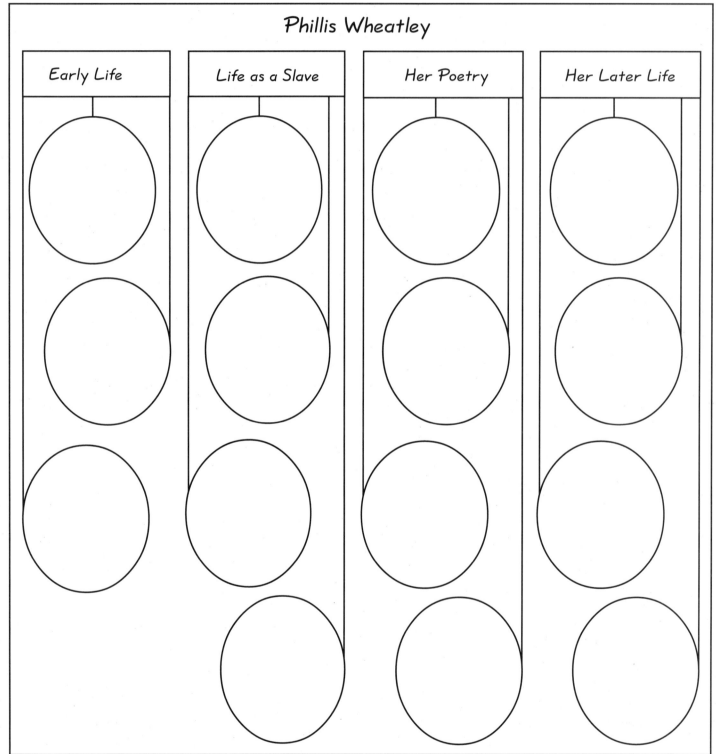

Phillis Wheatley

| Early Life | Life as a Slave | Her Poetry | Her Later Life |

Putting It All Together

Use your completed information map to write an outline about Phillis Wheatley.

Phillis Wheatley

I. _____
   A. _____
   B. _____
   C. _____

II. _____
   A. _____
   B. _____
   C. _____
   D. _____

III. _____
   A. _____
   B. _____
   C. _____
   D. _____

IV. _____
   A. _____
   B. _____
   C. _____
   D. _____

Challenge

• Using your outline about Phillis Wheatley as a guide, tell a group of students in another class about her life.

• Use the outline about the echidna to write a short report.

Name:

Using Several References

Sometimes the book or story you are reading does not answer all your questions. Then you need to read more than one book or story to find the answers.

Salvatore Student is going to the Hawaiian Islands for a vacation. He will spend time on the island of Hawaii. The only thing he knows about the island is that it is called "The Big Island." His friend Serena thinks there may be volcanoes there. Salvatore thinks he will enjoy his trip more if he learns more about the island before the trip. Here are the questions he wants to answer:

• Why is Hawaii called "The Big Island"?

• Are there volcanoes on the island of Hawaii?

Salvatore came home from the library with three books. Read the information he found and help him complete his notes and outline.

Island Geography

The Hawaiian Islands are a chain of islands located in the Pacific Ocean 2,000 miles from California. There are eight large islands and many small ones. The islands were formed by ancient volcanoes.

Hawaii is the youngest and largest of the islands. It's about 500,000 years old. Kauai, the oldest, is about 6 million years old.

Hawaii

The Hawaiian Islands are made up of 8 large islands and 124 small islands and reefs. The islands were formed by the lava flow from volcanoes.

There are five volcanoes on the island of Hawaii. Two of the volcanoes, Mauna Loa and Kilauea, are active. Kilauea is located on the southeastern edge of Hawaii Volcanoes National Park. Mauna Loa can be seen in the northwestern section of the same park.

Name: _____

Using Several References

Hawaii's Tall Volcano

Mauna Kea on the island of Hawaii is the world's highest volcano. It rises 33,476 feet from the bottom of the ocean floor. It doesn't look as tall as it really is. Only 13,796 feet of Mauna Kea is above sea level. There are pockets of snow near the top or summit.

Here are Salvatore's notes. His mother called him to dinner before he finished writing details about Mauna Kea.

📖 **Finish the notes for him.**

Why is Hawaii called "The Big Island"?

  largest of 8 large islands

Are there volcanoes on the island of Hawaii?

   Five volcanoes on Hawaii

   Mauna Loa and Kilauea are active

   Kilauea is on southeastern edge of Hawaii Volcanoes
      National Park

   Mauna Loa is on northwestern side of the park

   Mauna Kea is the world's highest volcano

_____

_____

_____

Using Several References

Use the notes to complete Salvatore's outline.

The Island of Hawaii

I. Biggest of the Hawaiian Islands

II. Volcanoes on the island

    A. Kilauea

        1. active

        2. southeastern edge of Hawaii Volcanoes

           National Park

    B. Mauna Loa

        1. _____

        2. northwestern side of Hawaii Volcanoes

           National Park

    C. Mauna Kea

        1. _____

        2. _____

        3. _____

        4. _____

Name:

Your Review Guide

Reading Nonfiction

Many times you will want to read a nonfiction book for fun. You won't be looking for key words or writing main ideas and details. Often, however, you have a special reason for looking up information. You need to remember and write about what you read.

The following list is a review of different ways to remember and write about nonfiction. You can use the list as a guide when you need to write a report or find information for a school project.

1.   Before you read, write questions about what you want to know.

2.   Read. Write the main ideas. (You can use the answers to the questions as the main ideas, or use the main ideas of the paragraphs you read.)

3.   Map the main ideas under the topic or title.

4.   Write the important details that tell about the main ideas.

5.   Map the details under the main ideas.

6.   Using the map, write an outline. The map and outline put the information in order so that you can tell or write about what you have read.

Writing Your Story

Remember, it's important not to copy information from a book word for word. Many stories are copyrighted. That means the person who wrote the article, or the publisher who printed it, owns the story. An outline helps you write information in your own words.

Every person has a special way of telling a story. It's important that you share your story your way.

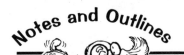

Name: _____

Outline Form

_____

I. _____

   A. _____

   B. _____

   C. _____

II. _____

   A. _____

   B. _____

   C. _____

III. _____

   A. _____

   B. _____

   C. _____

IV. _____

   A. _____

   B. _____

   C. _____

Evaluating Information

This chapter will help students think about and evaluate what they read.

Extra! Extra!
After completing page 44, have groups of students write a question about information in a science or social science book. They then write three facts. One of the facts doesn't answer the question. For example:

What do octopuses eat?
- **1.** Octopuses eat lobsters.
- **2.** Octopuses eat crabs.
- **3.** Octopuses eat the wood on piers.

Groups challenge each other to find the fact that doesn't answer the question.

Reading Between the Lines
To introduce this skill, you may wish to reproduce page 47 on a transparency rather than copying the page for each student.

Summarizing Practice
- **1.** Have students write new headlines for the articles in the section.
- **2.** Brainstorm titles for sections in social science and science books.
- **3.** Cut out short newspaper articles without the headlines. Ask students to write titles for the articles.

Transformation
The activity on page 59 asks students to write a poem based on an information article. This is a difficult task. You may choose to do this as a class or in small groups.

Review with the students the stories and activities they have done in this book. Point out the ways they transformed or changed the information in the stories. They can make information reports by drawing pictures or posters, making charts and diagrams, and writing poems. This will produce exciting science and social science displays for the classroom.

Name:

Extra! Extra! Read All About It!

Sometimes the details you read are interesting, but they don't fit under your main ideas or answer questions about your subject. Here are two exercises to help you eliminate information that does not fit under the main ideas.

📖 **Decide which of the facts below fit under the main idea, Parts of a Leaf. Cross out the details that don't belong.**

Parts of a Leaf

a blade is the broad flat part of the leaf
roots are another part of the plant
the stem of the leaf is called the petiole
a bulb is an underground stem
leaves have many sizes and shapes
tubes or veins in the leaf carry water and
    dissolved mineral food
other tubes take food away from the leaf
the midrib is the middle of the leaf

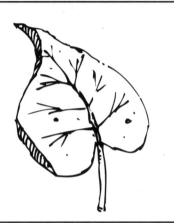

📖 **Help Sidney Student edit his report about the octopus. Draw a line through the information in the article that doesn't tell about the octopus.**

The Octopus

The octopus lives in the sea. It's a member of the mollusk family, but it doesn't have shell armor to protect its body. Clams are mollusks that have two shells. The octopus has no backbone. Its mouth has a horny beak. Many sea animals can be found on the ocean floor. The octopus has eight tentacles with suction-cup disks that can grip its prey. Its relative the squid has ten tentacles. Some, like the Pacific octopus, grow up to 30 feet in diameter. Others are only two to three inches across. Slugs are an example of land molluks.

Using its beak, the octopus can crush the shells of lobsters and crabs for a seafood dinner. It can wiggle a tentacle so it looks like a tasty worm. Curious fish that swim by to take a look end up inside the octopus. The shipworm is a mollusk with a different menu. It eats into the wood on piers and boats.

When threatened, the octopus lets off a dark, cloudy liquid and jets away. Squids shoot out a dark liquid, too. A soft body allows the octopus to squeeze into small spaces between rocks. The rocks in the sea also serve as hideouts for the moray eel. There the octopus is safe from other sea creatures looking for a soft meal.

The octopus can see trouble coming. It has good eyesight, even in deep water. For more protection, this clever sea creature can change color to blend in with its ocean hideaway. Squids often swim in large schools for protection.

How to Read Nonfiction Books EMC 572

Name: _____

Sequencing Information

1

The events in stories are not always written in chronological (by time - first, second, third, etc.) order. You must read carefully to decide the order of events in a story.

The following sentences are from a biography about George Catlin, who painted pictures of Native Americans during the late 1800s.

Number the sentences chronologically from 1 to 7. Some of the details are numbered for you.

George Catlin

_1_ George Catlin was born in 1796.

_7_ He died in 1872.

____ He did not like being a lawyer so he began painting pictures of people.

____ When he was a young man, he became an apprentice to a lawyer to learn about laws.

____ Today, his paintings and journals are important records that show how Native Americans lived in the 1800s.

_3_ He opened his own law practice in Pennsylvania.

_5_ He decided to travel with his sketch brushes and paints to American Indian settlements in the west.

____ He spent the rest of his life painting and writing about North and South American Indians.

How to Read Nonfiction Books EMC 572

Name: _____

More Sequencing Practice

After an entire school year of fund-raising, Steve Student's class is finally ready for the big field trip. Steve decided to write about the experience. Unfortunately, all his note cards got mixed up. Help Steve get his notes in order so that he can write his report.

📖 **Number the following events chronologically.**

📖 **Fill in the words in the last sentence to tell where the class is going. It should be the best field trip you can imagine.**

_____ I stuffed everything I needed into my backpack, including my lunch, a day's supply of peanut clusters, and a bottle of water.

_____ Sammy was my seat partner on the train.

_____ The two sixth-grade classes had a whole coach all to themselves.

_____ I walked to the train depot where I met the other students in the class.

_____ The sixth-grade classes had been raising money for the big June field trip all year.

_____ The conductor helped us on the train.

_____ Sammy sold the most holiday candles, and I sold the most peanut clusters.

_____ The teacher checked off our names and handed us our tickets.

_____ It was a two-hour ride to_____

Challenge

Write a paragraph with at least three sentences about the rest of the field trip. Write the sentences in chronological order.

_____

_____

_____

_____

_____

_____

_____

Name:

Reading Between the Lines

Thinking about what you read is just as important as finding facts in a story. Sometimes the information you read does not answer your question directly, but you can figure out the answer by putting together "clues" from the story. This is called **drawing conclusions**. Here is an example:

You are trying to find out which place in the United States has recorded the hottest temperature. In the Almanac you read:

> The world temperature record is held by El Azizia, Libya. On September 13, 1922 the recorded temperature was 136.4°F. Death Valley, California, registered the second highest temperature of 134° F for second place in July in 1913.

You can draw a conclusion from these facts:

If the country of Libya holds the world's first place record and Death Valley in the United States the second, no other place in the United States would have a higher temperature. Therefore, even though it doesn't say that Death Valley has the highest recorded temperature in the United States, you know no other place has recorded a higher temperature.

From the information you conclude that the highest recorded temperature in the United States was in Death Valley.

Name: _____

Practice Drawing Conclusions

1

Read the following stories. At the end of the first two selections, put an X in front of the conclusion that can be made from the information in the story. For the third selection, you will write your own conclusion.

The Flat-Headed Frog

The flat-headed frog lives in the Australian desert. When water is available, it absorbs water through its skin. It drinks large quantities of water when it can. The frog's body swells to resemble a round ball when filled with water. During the dry season when it's very hot, the frog, bloated with water, tunnels under the ground to stay cool.

_____ The flat-headed frog can survive without water for long periods of time.

_____ The flat-headed frog drinks too much water.

School Daze

Thursday after school, Alice watched two movies on TV. Her science report on spiders was due the next day. She didn't worry because she had written half of it on Tuesday. She planned to finish the rest of the report the next morning before she went to school. Accidently, Alice set her alarm for 6:00 P.M. instead of 6:00 A.M. She didn't wake up until 7:15 A.M. She had 30 minutes to get ready for school and eat breakfast.

_____ Alice didn't have enough time to finish her science report Friday morning.

_____ Reports about birds are more interesting than spider reports.

Manatees

The manatee is an endangered animal. Sometimes known as the seacow, this gentle animal does not harm others. Many manatees are killed or seriously injured when they are hit by motorboats. Laws limit the use of motorboats in areas where manatees can be found, but accidents continue to happen.

The manatee feeds on seagrass along the coast and near rivers. Many people have moved to Florida and crowded into areas where manatees live. Some of the feeding areas are destroyed when houses and businesses are built along the shore. Today there are less than1800 manatees living along the coastal areas of the United States.

Conclusion _____

_____

_____

Name:

Drawing Conclusions

2

📖 **Read the following story about Jane Addams, a pioneer in caring for the poor. At the end of the story write a conclusion about her work that isn't given in the story.**

Jane Addams 1860-1935

Jane Addams opened a settlement house in Chicago to help poor people. Many were immigrants who had come from other countries. The house was called Hull House.

Jane came from a wealthy family, but she suffered from a crooked back as a child. She felt ugly and was unable to do many things other children could do. She decided to help others when she grew up.

At Hull House she helped mothers learn better ways to care for their children. She aided the sick and helped people find decent places to live. She showed them how to cook nourishing foods.

Jane and her friend Ellen Starr set up an art gallery and provided books and magazines for people who visited Hull House. They felt that poor people who worked long hours under poor conditions should enjoy beauty. The art and reading rooms were a great success. They added a music school. There was a room for older members of the family to work on crafts. They made carvings and sewn items they could sell for money.

Jane set up a playground for children so they wouldn't have to play in the streets. There was a nursery school where working mothers could leave their children during the day.

_____

_____

_____

_____

_____

_____

Summarizing What You Read

Do you ever read a TV magazine or newspaper to see what a program is going to be about? Have you read what a book jacket says a story is about before deciding to check out the book? Both of these are examples of **summaries.**

A summary tells the most important ideas of an article or story in a very brief way. Even when you are reading for fun, try to summarize what you have read.

📖 **Read the following two paragraphs. Ask yourself, "What is the paragraph about?" For each paragraph, choose the sentence that you think best summarizes the information.**

Spider Webs

Each kind of spider has a special web shape. Orb weavers spin round webs. Grass spiders build webs that are shaped like funnels. A purse-web spider spins a long tube. A comb-footed spider builds a hanging bell-shaped web. These special webs are used to trap insects. Some also serve as homes for the spider.

_____ Spider webs trap insects.
_____ Spider webs come in many shapes and uses.
_____ Grass spiders build funnel-shaped webs.

Central Park

Five hundred people attended the opening of the new park in Central City. The lake was ready for canoes and kayaks. There are two play areas, one for young children and another with twisting slides and tunnels for older children. Green trees, grass, and a small stream with several families of ducks will attract weekend crowds with picnic lunches.

The mayor cut the ribbon for the new park. In his speech he said, "This beautiful park is for everyone in Central City. Children will have a place to play, and families can enjoy time outdoors together."

After his speech the mayor and the city workers who built the park jogged the two miles around the lake.

_____ Central Park offers many choices for recreational activities.
_____ Central Park was created recently.
_____ Children will have a lot to do in Central Park.

Writing Summaries

2

Sally Student was trying to decide if she wanted to spend the money to see the movie Go West Young Spaniel. She knew that Samantha had seen it, so she asked Samantha to tell her about the story. Forty-five minutes later, Sally had heard every detail of the movie and was bored to tears. Poor Samantha - no one ever taught her how to summarize!

How are your summarization skills? Read the following selections and follow the instructions.

Alberta, Canada

There are many scenic places for tourists to see in Alberta, Canada. The Rocky Mountains, many national parks, and wilderness areas are visited by millions of people every year. Banff National Park is a favorite tourist stop. Dinosaur Provincial Park and the Royal Tyrrell Museum draw many visitors who want to know more about these fascinating prehistoric animals.

Write a slogan for a travel advertisement that summarizes the paragraph.

_____

_____

_____

Venus's-Flytrap

A very strange plant grows in North Carolina. It eats insects! It is called Venus's-flytrap because it traps insects. There is not enough food in the soil where this plant grows, so the flytrap catches insects to eat.

This strange plant has leaves that work like a steel trap. The two halves of the leaf are hinged in the middle. When an insect lands on it, the leaf closes and traps the insect. Juices in the plant digest the insect.

Write a summary of no more than two sentences.

_____

_____

_____

Name: _____

1

Learning to Generalize

When you **generalize**, you form an opinion about the information you have read. Often that opinion, or general statement, is about a whole group of people, animals, events, or places. Here are some examples from selections you have read:

After reading about spiders you could generalize that spiders spend a lot of time weaving webs.

When you read about Alberta, Canada, you could make the general statement that Alberta is a good place for tourists to visit.

When you read the story School Daze you could generalize that it's better to finish homework before watching TV.

📖 **Read the following paragraph about monkeys.**

📖 **Choose the statement that a person could generalize after reading the paragraph.**

Monkeys are very nosy and lively. They like to learn how things are made. They will often take things apart. A monkey can't resist finding out what is inside a package. Monkeys like to swing and jump from place to place. They need lots of space to climb.

_____ Monkeys are fun to watch.
_____ Monkeys would make a mess in your kitchen.
_____ A monkey would not make a good pet.

Beginning below are three stories about the marsh mosquito. Even though just facts are used, each paragraph presents a different opinion about the mosquito.

📖 **Read each paragraph**

📖 **Write a generalization for each paragraph.**

The Marsh Mosquito

The Anderson Marsh is a breeding ground for mosquitoes. The large marsh mosquitoes are attacking animals and people in the nearby community of Andersonville. The mosquitoes carry diseases and cause great discomfort. The city council will vote on Tuesday on whether to drain the marsh and rid the city of this pest.

Generalization: _____

_____

Name: _____

Learning to Generalize

2

The Marsh Mosquito

Many birds who call Anderson Marsh home depend on the marsh mosquito larvae for their food. Each year they visit the marsh and build their nests. They feed themselves and their young on small insects and larvae found in the marsh. The frogs, toads, and fish in the marsh also depend on the larvae for food.

Generalization: _____

_____

Mosquito Control

Many mosquitoes in Andersonville do not come from the marsh. Gardeners save rain water in barrels and jugs for their gardens. Large numbers of mosquitoes are breeding in the open water containers.

Generalization: _____

_____

Notice that the information a writer includes in a story can change the way a reader thinks about a subject. Writers can change your ideas by including some facts and leaving out others. It's important to read more than one story about a subject before you form opinions or generalize.

📖 **Write one general statement about mosquitoes that is based on the information in all three stories.**

_____

_____

_____

Name:

Transformation

When you made an information map or outline from the facts in a story, you transformed or changed the form of what you read.

There are many ways to transform information.

📖 **You can picture facts. You can show the stages of a frog's life cycle with pictures.**

📖 **You can make a chart that is easily understood.**

Butterfly Metamorphosis

 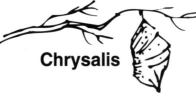 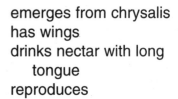

Larva	**Chrysalis**	**Adult**
hatches from egg	spun from silk	emerges from chrysalis
worm-like	turns hard	has wings
eats constantly	attaches to a stem	drinks nectar with long tongue
		reproduces

📖 **You can put the information in a poem or poster. The following poem is from the information on spiders. Draw spider pictures around the poem.**

Spider Webs

Round, funnel, tubes, and bell—
The spider weaves a magic spell.
A place to stay,
A net for prey,
The spider's web serves very well.

Transforming an Article to a Picture

Articles that tell you the steps of a process are good ones to transform to pictures. In fact, this is often the clearest way to communicate a process to your audience.

📖 **Read this selection about how bread is made.**

📖 **Decide on the six most important ideas to show.**

📖 **Draw the six ideas in the boxes below.**

Wheat, harvested by machines, is taken to mills to be ground into flour. Bakeries purchase large bags of flour from the flour mills. At the bakery, ingredients such as flour, salt, sugar, yeast, water, and eggs are blended together in large mixers. The dough is shaped into loaves and left to rise before baking. After baking, the fresh bread is wrapped and sent to the store. Now you can fix your favorite sandwich.

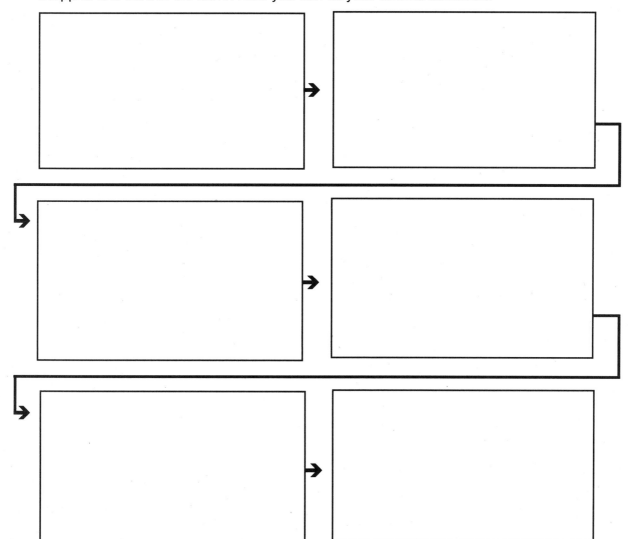

Name:

Transforming an Article into a Chart

3

Sidney Student decided to take his report and display the infomation in a chart form. He left out a few details. Read Sidney's report again and add details to the chart. The numbers in parenthesis tell you how many details to add.

The Octopus

The octopus lives in the sea. It's a member of the mollusk family, but it doesn't have shell armor to protect its body. The octopus has no backbone. Its mouth has a horny beak. The octopus has eight tentacles with suction-cup disks that can grip its prey. Some, like the Pacific octopus, grow up to 30 feet in diameter. Others are only two to three inches.

Using its beak, the octopus can crush the shells of lobsters and crabs for a seafood dinner. It can wiggle a tentacle so it looks like a tasty worm. Curious fish that swim by to take a look end up inside the octopus.

When threatened, the octopus lets off a dark, cloudy liquid and jets away. A soft body allows the octopus to squeeze into small spaces between rocks. There the octopus is safe from other sea creatures looking for a soft meal.

The octopus can see trouble coming. It has good eyesight, even in deep water. For more protection, this clever sea creature can change color to blend in with its ocean hideaway.

The Octopus			
Protection (1)	**Body (2)**	**Food (1)**	**Size (1)**
lets off dark liquid before escaping soft body squeezes into tight spaces good eyesight spots trouble	soft no backbone suction discs	beak crushes shells of lobsters and crabs for seafood meal	some only two to three inches in diameter

Name:

A Charting Challenge

4

Get together with one to three classmates. Choose a sport you enjoy watching or playing.

On the form below, make a chart for the sport. Suggested column headings, are **Equipment**, **Players**, **Scoring**, **General Rules**. You can add more columns or remove any columns from this list.

Name of Sport			

Chart Form

Name:

Transforming an Article to a Poem

5

📖 **Read the following paragraphs about the sun. Using some of the information in the story, write a poem about the sun.**

Here are some ideas to help you:
- Form a picture in your mind about the sun and use a word to communicate what you "see."
- Your poem does not have to rhyme.
- If you have learned to write cinquain verse, you might use that form.
- Include several facts.
- Use words that are pleasing to the ear.

The Sun

The sun is our closest star. The sun is made up of gasses. The temperature on the surface of the sun is about 5,800 degrees Centigrade. Anything coming close to the sun would burn up from the heat.

Atomic particles, light, and radio waves are let off by the sun. Most ultraviolet light from the sun is filtered out in the atmosphere before it reaches the earth. Ultraviolet light can be used to kill germs, but too much of it can harm animals and plants.

Solar heat affects the climate and oceans on earth. Heat from the sun evaporates water into the air. About 500 trillion tons of water on earth evaporate every year. When the water falls back on the earth, it helps plants grow. Heat from the sun heats the air. Winds develop from the movement of cool and warm air. Currents in the ocean are caused by solar heat.

Most plants need sunlight to grow. Plants change carbon dioxide and sunlight into sugar and starch. This solar-made food helps the plants grow the leaves and fruit that we eat.

Checklist of Skills ✓

	Students' Names									
Uses prereading questions to locate important facts when reading about:										
events										
animals										
biographies										
Uses a traditional or electronic card catalog to locate information in the library										
Uses a table of contents and index to locate specific information										
Uses key words to scan for information										
Creates an information map using main ideas and details										
Takes notes using only necessary words										
Creates a simple outline of main ideas and details from notes or an information map										
Recognizes extraneous detail in an information article										
Puts events in chronological order										
Draws logical conclusions from information read										
Summarizes information read										
Generalizes to form an opinion about information read										
Reports information using a variety of forms										
pictures										
poem										
chart										
Shows interest in learning new reading skills for accessing information										
Shows interest in reading nonfiction for own purposes										

Answer Key

Note: many answers given are just samples. Student answers will often vary. Any reasonable answer should be accepted.

Page 2
1. Who burned the White House?
   English toops under General Ross and Admiral Cockburn
2. What happened?
   Soldiers piled everything in the middle of the rooms; set things on fire; gunpowder exploded; White House was destoyed.
3. Where did the White House burn?
   In Washington City.
4. When did the White House burn?
   August 24, 1814
5. Why was the White House burned?
   The United States and Great Britain were at war because...

Page 4
1. cuckoo family
2. loose feathers, strong bill, tail longer than body, 1st & 4th toes point backward, brown & buff, line on cheek blue to orange
3. rattlesnakes, grasshoppers, birds' eggs, centipedes, scorpions, tarantulas, horned toads, mice, small rats, fruits, seeds, lizards.
4. desert
5. nests in high spot in cactus or bushes; made of snake skins, sticks, dry manure flakes, feathers
6. X
7. X
8. hunts rattlesnakes, likes walking better than flying

Page 5
(First word in the sentence and the number)
Matthew - 1
His mother - 3
He moved - 3
His uncle - 3, 4
At thirteen - 3
The captain - 4
He traveled - 4
Wherever - 4
Later - 5
Finally - 5
He was - 5
Peary - 5

Page 5 (continued)
In June - 5
They explored - 5
Henson was a valuable - 5
He worked - 5
Henson was the co-discoverer - 5

Page 11
1. There is a list with the last names of the authors, another one with book titles, and a list of subjects.
2. (Circled) use letters for different subjects
3. (Boxed) has a system of numbers.
4. (A triangle in front of) Biographies and autobiographies are shelved alphabetically by the person's last name.

1. Dewey Decimal System
2. microfilm and microfiche
3. by author, book title, and subject
4. Reference section

Page 13
1. Chapter 3
2. Chapter 6
3. Chapter 5
4. Chapter 4, 5
5. Chapter 2
6. Chapter 4
Inside the Chapter
1. Chapter 4
2. Chapter 6
3. Chapter 5

Page 14
1. 14, 26
2. 7, 15–18
3. 8, 18–20
4. 14
5. 1–2, 12, 16, 27
6. 1–2, 13, 15, 26

Page 15
The echidna is a spiny anteater that lives in Australia. (This sentence is to be circled)
(The following is to be underlined.)
long, thin snout, small mouth, short legs, spines on back and sides; brow; Between its spines it has stiff hairs, toes on hindfeet with long claws.

Answer Key

Page 16
1. Sam Martin
2. <u>final score</u>, Washington 41   Barkley 7
3. <u>touchdowns</u>, <u>Washinton</u>, <u>last quarter</u>, two
4. <u>name</u>, <u>Washington</u>, <u>team</u>, Scorpions
5. <u>caught</u> <u>five</u> <u>passes</u>, Alan Baker

Page 17
1. age 10
2. fireman for the railroad
3. mechanical engineering
4. <u>Bell Telephone</u>, telephone transmitter
5. <u>improve train safety</u>, developed a train telegraph system so moving trains would know when another train was on the track
6. <u>brakes</u>, automatic air brakes

Page 20
2. The Amazon has more tributaries than any other river in the world.
3. Each day the Amazon deposits tons of food-laden silt in the ocean.

Page 22

Black Bears

| |
| Black bears are the smallest bears in North America. |
| Black bears are ominvores. |

Page 23

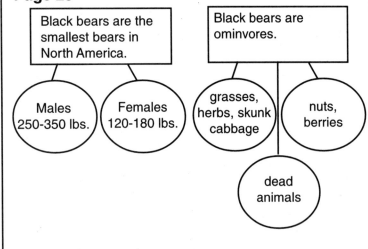

Black bears are the smallest bears in North America.

Males 250-350 lbs.

Females 120-180 lbs.

Black bears are ominvores.

grasses, herbs, skunk cabbage

nuts, berries

dead animals

Page 28
1. X born in 1867
8. X patients mistreated, many didn't belong there
11. X traveled by ship, train, sampan, horse, butto, stagecoach, jinricksha
12. X returned in 72 days, 6 hours, 11 minutes, and 14 seconds
13. X married millionaire, Robert Seaman, 1895
14-16 may include:
    ran his manufacturing plant after he died, business failed, interned in Europe during World War I, died January 27, 1922

Page 29
2. Sojourner Truth spoke against slavery, visited President Lincoln
3. Moon smaller than Earth, grayish rocks, dust
4. Koalas, "no drink" in Aborigine, eucalyptus forests NE, SE Australia coast.
5. peanuts - tasty, healthful, used in soap, face powder, shaving cream, shampoo, paint
6. Columbus - sail around globe to prove earth sphere, not flat
7. rhinoceros rests in day, active at night, eats grass, twigs, shrubs

Page 30
1. made of ice, dirt, and rock
2. coma (tail) is gas.
3. coma (tail) million miles long
4. lose dust and gas, get smaller
5. some visit sun once, others return
6. Halley's every 76 years
7. Hally's next trip 2061

Page 32
The eruption of Mount St. Helens on May 18, 1980, caused widespread destruction = 4, 5, 6

Signs of the explosion traveled long. distances=1, 2, 3

7 and 8
    Answers will vary

Answer Key

Page 34
Order may vary.
A. Digs up nests and homes of insects
B. Pulls out insects with long, sticky tongue
C. Crushes food in mouth - no teeth
D. Grains of dirt it scoops up help grind its food

Page 36
The details on page 35 should be written in the circles under the same heading.

Page 37
I. Early life
   A. Born in Africa
   B. Captured, brought to America as a slave when 8 or 9
   C. Bought by John Wheatley in Boston
II. Life as a slave
   A. Companion for twins, Mary and Nathaniel
   B. Helped Mrs. Wheatley, an invalid
   C. Taught to read and write
   D. Given freedom in 1772 when about 20
III. Her poetry
   A. Wrote first poem at age 13
   B. Wrote poem for Mary's Wedding
   C. People in Boston wanted poems written for them.
   D. Traveled to England where her poems were
      published, 1773
IV. Her later life
   A. Married John Peters
   B. Had three children, two died
   C. Husband taken to debtor's prison
   D. She and her baby died in December 1784

Page 39
Mauna Kea world's highest volcano
   rises 33,476 feet from ocean floor
   only 13,796 feet is above sea level
   snow near the summit

Page 40
B.
   1. active
C.
   1. world's highest volcano
   2. rises 33,476 feet from ocean floor
   3. 13,796 feet above sea level
   4. snow near summit

Answer Key

Page 44
Part of a Leaf
roots are another part of the plant
a bulb is an underground stem
leaves have many sizes and shapes

The Octopus
Clams are mollusks that have two shells
Many sea animals can be found on the ocean floor
Its relative the squid has ten tentacles
Slugs are an example of land mollusks
The shipworm is a mollusk with a different menu
It eats into the wood on piers and boats
Squids shoot out a dark liquid, too
The rocks in the sea also serve as hideouts for the
    moray eel
Squids often swim in large schools for protection.

Page 45
1, 7, 4, 2, 8, 3, 5, 6

Page 46
3, 8, 7, 4, 1, 6, 2, 5, 9

Page 48
The flat-headed frog can survive without water for
long periods of time.

Alice didn't have enough time to finish her science
report Friday morning.

Selection three - answers will vary. For example, if
manatees are not protected, they could become
extinct.

Page 49
(Sample answer)
Many people led better lives because of Jane
Addams' work at Hull House.

Page 50
Spider webs have many shapes and uses.

Central Park offers many choices for recreational
activities.

Page 51
Sample answer: Alberta Canada has many
interesting places to see.
Sample answer: Venus'-flytrap is a strange plant
that grows in North Carolina. Because the soil
doesn't have enough food in it, the plant traps and
digests insects.

Page 52
A Monkey would not make a good pet.

The Marsh Mosquito sample answer: The marsh
mosquito is a health problem.

Page 53
The Marsh Mosquito sample answer: Birds and
animals in the marsh need the marsh mosquito to
survive.
Mosquito Control sample answer: If water storage
containers were closed there wouldn't be as many
mosquitoes.

Generalizaiton from all 3 articles, sample answer:
The marsh mosquito will not be as big a problem if
there are enough birds and animals in the marsh
to eat them and people cover their water
containers.

Page 56

Protection	Body	Food	Size
	horny beak	eats fish	grows to 30 feet in diameter
changes color	eight tentacles		